2015

Marie Elen

Ugly would be so honored for you to leave this —

Sent With Love

Connie

TRANSACTIONAL THERAPY

WHEN THE BUTTERFLY
RESTS IN YOUR HAND
DO NOT CLOSE IT

SECOND EDITION
ROBERT M. ANTHONY, PH.D.
WITH
J. DIGBY HENRY, MA.

ZEN TRANSACTIONAL THERAPY

TABLE OF CONTENTS

ZTT . . . . ZEN TRANSACTIONAL THERAPY

ZEN . . . . THE ACTIVE PROCESS
OF UNIFICATION
OF THE PERSON
WITH ALL-THAT-IS,
WHERE NO THING
AND NO ONE
HAS ANY MORE IMPORTANCE
THEN ANY THING
OR ANY ONE ELSE.

TRANSACTIONAL . . . . THE CREATIVE INTERPLAY
OF THE WORLD
WITH THE WORLD,
WHEREIN ALL ARE EFFECTED
BY THE PLAY
AND ITS CONSEQUENCES

THERAPY . . . . THE ENRICHMENT
OF ALL PERSONS
AND THEIR LIVES
THROUGH HUMORFUL PLAY,
CREATIVE GAMING,
TENSION EXPLORATION,
SOCIOINSPECTION
AND PREFERENTIAL RELATING,
WHEREIN EACH PERSON
IS A PRIORITY
OVER ALL ELSE.

EVERYTHING
IS DONE
WITHIN ZTT.
IT IS A CRUCIBLE
OF CREATIVE LIFE.

RATHER THAN
LIVING LIFE
AND PLAYING ZTT,
ONE PLAYS LIFE
AND LIVES ZTT.

6

INTRODUCTION.

THIS BOOK
IS NOT ABOUT
ANY THING
OR ANY ONE.

IT IS A CREATION
AND A REFLECTION
OF
ZEN TRANSACTIONAL THERAPY (ZTT).

OFFERED
IN MEMORY OF
NO ONE,
DEDICATED TO
NO ONE,
WRITTEN FOR
NO ONE,

WITH A PREMISE
THAT WHATEVER
YOU TAKE SERIOUSLY
IS YOUR MASTER,
AND WHATEVER
YOU MASTER
HAS NO NEED
OF YOUR SERIOUSNESS,

WE PRESENT THIS
TO YOU
GENTLY,
AS A KOAN
TO BE SOLVED,
WITH A SMILE
AND LAUGHTER.

ROBERT M. ANTHONY, Ph.D.
J. DIGBY HENRY, M.A.

FOREWORD.

OUT OF NEEDS
FOR BEGINNINGS
WE CREATE GODS.

WITH DESIRES
FOR IMMORTALITY
WE ENTHRONE THEM.

IN AVOIDANCE OF SPONTANEITY
WE OBEY THEM.

IN FEAR
OF RISK
WE FOLLOW THEM.

FROM REJECTION
OF RESPONSIBILITY
WE WORSHIP THEM.

THIS IS
A PRE-TENSION
PROTECTING US
FROM THE TENSION
AND CONSEQUENCES
OF OUR CHOICE
AND ACTION.

WE MUST LEARN
NOW
TO ENSPIRIT
OUR LIVES
AND LIVE
OUR DEITY.

8

A ZZT MASTER.

A ZZT MASTER
IS A LIVING PORTRAIT
OF ALL THAT FULFILLS YOUR FEAR
OF BEING SPONTANEOUS.

> BOTH BEACON
> AND SIGNPOST,
> TWINKLING WITH LAUGHTER,
> DANCING IN YOUR PATH,
> THE ZTT MASTER PLAYS LIFE
> IN ITS FULLEST.
>
> IN WORDS AND ACTION,
> THE ZTT MASTER
> INVADES YOUR VICTIMHOOD
> WITH AN INVITATION
> TO PLAY
> BEYOND THE BOUNDARIES
> OF YOUR OWN DRAMA.

THE ZTT MASTER
SEEKS NO FOLLOWERS
AND DOES NOT DICTATE.

POSSESSING NO ONE
AND SUBJUGATING NO THING,
THE MASTER
IMPOSES NEITHER
HIMSELF
NOR ZTT
UPON
ANYTHING
ANYONE
OR
ANY
ONE.

THE PILGRIM

A PILGRIM CAME TO THE MASTER ASKING,
"HOW CAN I DISCOVER WHO I AM?"

EYES TWINKLING AND LAUGHING, THE
MASTER REPLIED, "WHEN YOU FIND THE
DIFFERENCE BETWEEN AN APPLE, YOU
WILL DISCOVER WHO YOU ARE."

THE PRINCIPLE
OF
INFINITE IDENTITY

ANOTHER PILGRIM CAME TO THE MASTER
SAYING, "I DON'T KNOW WHAT IS WRONG.
I AM NOT MYSELF TODAY."

"THEN," SAID THE MASTER, "SINCE YOU
ARE NOT YOU, TO WHOM AM I SPEAKING?"

A PICTURE FRAME
SERVES A TWOFOLD PURPOSE:
TO INCLUDE
ALL THAT IS
IN THE PICTURE
AND EXCLUDE
ALL ELSE.

THE FRAME
YOU PLACE
AROUND YOUR LIFE
DEFINES YOU
AND EXCLUDES
ALL THE POSSIBILITIES
OF WHO YOU ARE
AND WHO YOU CAN BE.

THE REACH
OF YOUR IDENTITY
INCLUDES
YOUR UNIQUE SELF
(CORE IDENTITY)
AND
ALL ELSE AROUND YOU
(CORPORATE IDENTITY).

THEREFORE,
YOUR ALLEGIANCES ARE
TO THE UNIVERSAL
AND
THE COSMIC.

TO GO IN SEARCH
OF YOUR IDENTITY
IS THE ABSURDITY
OF A MAN ON HORSEBACK
RIDING IN SEARCH
OF A HORSE.

YOUR IDENTITY INCLUDES
ALL THAT IS WITHIN
AND WITHOUT
YOURSELF.

EVERYONE
AND EVERYTHING
IS AN ASPECT
OF YOUR IDENTITY.

THEREFORE,
TREAT ALL
AS YOURSELF.

TO SAY
"THIS IS NOT ME"
IS AN ILLUSION OF WORDS
SUPPORTED BY
AN INSULAR IDENTITY.

WHEN YOU
ISOLATE
AND INSULATE
YOUR EXPERIENCE
FROM ALL OTHER EXPERIENCES,
SO YOU COUNTENANCE
THE MASQUERADE
OF LONELINESS.

THE NARCISSISTIC
INSULAR EGO
IS THE SERPENT
THAT SLITHERS
INTO THE SELF,
POISONING ITS WELL
OF COMPASSION
AND CONCERN
FOR OTHERS.

YOU ARE WHO YOU ARE.
YOU CANNOT BE NOT WHO YOU ARE,
EXCEPT AS YOU DECIDE TO CHANGE
WHO YOU ARE.

YOU ARE
PHYSIOLOGICALLY,
BIOLOGICALLY,
GENETICALLY,
HISTORICALLY,
SOCIALLY,
UNIQUE.

DO NOT WORRY
WHEN YOU INCORPORATE
THE EXPERIENCES OF THE OTHER
AS PART OF YOUR OWN IDENTITY.

YOU CANNOT LOSE
WHAT YOU CANNOT GIVE UP.

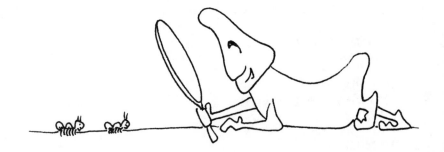

WHAT EVER YOU ARE DOING,
BECOME ONE WITH IT.

WHOM EVER YOU ARE WITH,
BECOME ONE WITH HIM.

WE ARE FOUR DIMENSIONAL CREATURES
OF VARIABLE
LENGTH, WIDTH, HEIGHT,
AND TIME.

WHO YOU ARE
AND WHO YOU ARE WITH
CHANGES
FROM MOMENT
TO MOMENT.

DO NOT CONCRETIZE
ANY IMPRESSION
OF YOURSELF
OR ANOTHER
AS THE FINAL
REPRESENTATION
OF WHO YOU
AND THEY
ARE.

WE ARE
GROWING,
MOVING,
CHANGING,
INTERPERSONAL ACTS
IN THE THEATER OF LIFE.

THE MORE YOU PRACTICE
THE ATTITUDE OF UNITY WITH OTHERS
THE MORE YOU WILL SENSE
THE EXPERIENCE OF UNITY.

THE EXPERIENCE OF UNITY
DOES NOT REQUIRE THAT
THE OTHER PERSON
HAVE THE SAME VISION.

HOWEVER, WHEN BOTH
EXPERIENCE UNITY
WITH EACH OTHER,
JOY
AND THE SENSE
OF CORPORATENESS
ENSUE.

OPEN
AND EXTEND
YOUR FAMILY
TO INCLUDE
ALL THE BEINGS
OF THIS EARTH
AND THE COSMOS.

REFLEXIVE
AND AUTOMATIC RESPONSES
ARE THE WALLS BETWEEN PEOPLE.

LEARN NOT TO ACT OUT
EVERY DISTRESSING FEELING
STIMULATED BY OTHERS.

WHEN NOT SUPPORTED IN ACTION,
THESE FEELINGS DISAPPEAR
IN THE FLOW
OF CHOICEFUL INTERACTION
OF MUTUALITY.

THIS IS A SOCIAL
EVOLUTIONARY STEP!

WITH EACH PERSON YOU ENCOUNTER,
MOVE TOWARD INTIMACY OF EXPERIENCE.
INTIMACY OF ACTION, HOWEVER,
REQUIRES MUTUAL AGREEMENT.

INTIMACY OF EXPERIENCE
IS THE PRODUCT OF MUTUALITY.
MUTUALITY ARISES
FROM THE ACTIVITY
OF EACH PERSON
EXPERIENCING THE OTHER
IN THE PRESENT MOMENT.

IN MUTUALITY:
I LOOK AT YOU
AND SEE YOU,
YOU LOOK AT ME
AND SEE ME.

IN PSEUDO-MUTUALITY:
I LOOK AT YOU
AND SEE YOU,
YOU LOOK AT YOU
AND SEE YOU,
OR
I LOOK AT ME
AND SEE ME,
YOU LOOK AT YOU
AND SEE YOU,
OR
I LOOK AT ME
AND SEE ME,
YOU LOOK AT ME
AND SEE ME.

IN INCOMPLETE MUTUALITY:
WE LOOK AT AN ISSUE
OR A CAUSE
AND CREATE THE ILLUSION
OF BEING TOGETHER.

INTIMACY OF ACTION
ATTENDS
TO MUTUAL AGREEMENT
TO ACT
ON THE BASIS
OF WHAT BOTH
SEE,
FEEL
AND WISH TO DO.

MUTUALITY
REQUIRES
THE COMMITMENT
TO PASSAGE
THE GAUNTLET
OF ONE'S OWN
VULNERABILITIES.

TO BRING YOURSELF
AND THE PERSON YOU ARE WITH
INTO THE PRESENT MOMENT,
FOCUS YOUR ATTENTION
WHOLLY ON THE OTHER,
BEING AWARE
OF WHAT YOU SENSE
OF WHAT YOU EXPERIENCE
OF WHAT YOU WISH TO DO.

THIS IS THE PROCESS
OF SOCIOINSPECTION.
WITH YOUR ATTENTION
FOCUSED ON THE OTHER,
COMPLETE THESE STATEMENTS:

"I SEE YOU .... (GIVE AN IMPRESSION)."

"I SEE YOU ...... AND FEEL TOWARD YOU ......"
(INCLUDE THOSE FEELINGS WHICH ARE BASED ON
YOUR IMPRESSIONS).

"I SEE YOU ... AND I FEEL TOWARD YOU ... AND
I WOULD LIKE ...."
(GIVE A STATEMENT OF DESIRED ACTION BASED
ON YOUR IMPRESSIONS AND FEELINGS).

AS YOUR IMPRESSION
OF ANOTHER
WILL CHANGE
MOMENT TO MOMENT,
SO WHAT YOU FEEL
AND WISH TO DO
WILL ALSO CHANGE.

26

SOCIOINSPECTION
IS THE ACTIVITY
OF TREATING
ONESELF AS GROUND
AND OTHERS
AS FIGURE.

BECOME SOCIOINSPECTIVE
IN YOUR RELATIONSHIPS.

ALLOW OTHERS
AND THEIR ISSUES
TO BECOME FIGURE
IN THE RESPONSE
WHERE YOU
ARE THE BACKGROUND.

ONLY IN THIS MANNER
CAN YOU TRULY
BE WITH ANOTHER.

DO NOT CONCRETIZE
YOUR EXPERIENCE.

DO NOT ATTACK
OR DEFEND
IMPRESSIONS,
FEELINGS,
OR DESIRED ACTIONS
WHEN WITH ANOTHER.

SUCH BEHAVIORS
SERVE ONLY
TO ISOLATE YOU
AND WARD OFF MUTUALITY.

LOOK TO YOUR CHILDREN!
THEY MIRROR
WHO YOU ARE,
WHAT YOU ARE,
HOW YOU ARE
AND WHAT YOU AVOID
IN THE WORLD.

YOU ARE A CRAFTSMAN
IN THE THEATER OF LIFE.

LEARN TO BE
AN EFFECTIVE MANIPULATOR.
TREAT YOURSELF
AND OTHERS
AS MOVING SCULPTURES
EVOLVING
INTO MORE COMPLEX FORMS.

SELF AWARENESS
IS A PROCESS
OF CHECKING IN
ON ONE'S SELF,
TAKING CARE
OF ONE'S SELF,
AND NOT ALLOWING
ONE'S SELF
TO INTERFERE
WITH ONE'S BLENDING
WITH ANOTHER.

TO BE FULLY WHO YOU ARE,
BECOME THE ACTOR
AND THE ACTRESS
AND PLAY OUT IN TOTAL
THE PERSON YOU WANT TO BE.

ACTION CHANGES BEING.

BEING AND BECOMING
ARE ONE
AND THE SAME.

NO PERSON
HAS MORE
OR LESS
VALUE
THAN ANY OTHER PERSON
IN THE UNIVERSE,
OR ANY LIVING ENTITY
IN THE UNIVERSE,
OR THE UNIVERSE.

IN A WORLD
WHERE ALL PERSONS
AND ALL THINGS
ARE EQUALLY IMPORTANT
PERSONS STILL HAVE PRIORITY.

WHEN THEY DO NOT
THEY ARE BRUTALIZED,
EACH BECOMING
SOME THING
INSTEAD OF
SOMEONE.

TO ACT IN PREFERENCE
AND PRIORITY
DOES NOT REQUIRE
THE DEVALUATION
OF THAT WHICH IS
NOT PREFERRED.

YOU AND I
ARE ONE FACET
OF ALL-THAT-IS·
ALL OTHERS
ARE FACETS
ALSO.

THEY ARE YOU.
YOU ARE THEY.

I/YOU/THEY/WE
ARE ALL
THAT IS:
ONE.

34

ALL-THAT-IS
IS ALL
THAT
IS.

ALL-THAT-IS
IS REFLECTED
EVERYWHERE,
IN EVERYONE
AND EVERYTHING.

ALL-THAT-IS
IS NOT EXCLUSIVE.

ALL-THAT-IS
IS,
WAS
AND
WILL BE
ALWAYS.

THE PRINCIPLE
OF
HUMORFUL PLAY

"THERE IS NO JOY IN MY LIFE,"
SAID THE PILGRIM. "SHOW ME
HOW I MAY FIND HAPPINESS."

THE MASTER SMILED .... AND
LAUGHED AND LAUGHED AND LAUGHED
AND LAUGHED AND LAUGHED AND LAUGHED.

EVERYTHING IS SACRED
AND TO BE LAUGHED AT
WITH THE IRREVERENT HUMOR
OF ONE FREE
OF THE FEAR
OF NOVELTY.

THE ONLY APPROPRIATE
RELIGIOUS RITUAL:
  LAUGHTER
  AT THE CARICATURES
  OF ONESELF,
  OTHERS
  AND PROBLEMS.

LAUGHTER
DISSOLVES
TUNNEL VISION
AND INCREASES
THE OPTIONS
OF CHOICE.

LEARN TO LAUGH
IN THE FACE OF SERIOUSNESS.
ACT HUMOROUSLY
WHERE SERIOUSNESS DIRECTS YOUR COURSE,
AND SERIOUSNESS WILL MELT
INTO A FLUID FREEDOM
OF JOYOUS EXPERIENCE.

SERIOUSNESS SETS THE CONCRETE
OR RIGID THINKING
AND REFLEXIVE ACTIVITY,
ETCHING BEHAVIOR
AND FEELING
INTO PATHWAYS
OF STONE AND MORTAR.

TO DISCOVER HUMOR
ACT WITH HUMOR
EVEN WHEN YOU DO NOT FEEL HUMOR.

LAUGHTER IS THE TRANSPORT
THROUGH THE BARRIERS
OF EMOTIONAL PAIN.

ZTT LAUGHTER
IS NEVER USED
FOR DERISION,
BUT FOR INCORPORATION
WITH ALL-THAT-IS.

COMPULSIVE EXPRESSIONS
OF STRONG EMOTION
ARE OFTEN CONFUSED
WITH SPONTANEITY.

SPONTANEITY
IS A LIGHT,
HUMOROUS,
CARING RESULT
OF HAVING LEARNED
TO ACT INDEPENDENTLY
OF BOTH NEGATIVE
AND POSITIVE
EMOTIONS.

SPONTANEITY RESULTS
FROM SELF-DISCIPLINE.

DISCIPLINE YOURSELF
TO PLAY HUMOROUSLY
AT HOME,
IN WORK,
AT PLAY.

EVERYWHERE
AND EVERYTHING
IS A PLAYGROUND
FOR HUMOR.

DISCIPLINE
WITHOUT JOY
IS FATAL.

BEWARE THE SERIOUSNESS OF OTHERS.
IT IS CONTAGEOUS AND ADDICTING.

IN SERIOUSNESS
YOU AUTOMATICALLY LOSE CONCERN
FOR MUTUAL ENRICHMENT,
BECOMING ENTRENCHED
IN AN IMPOVERISHED
INSULAR IDENTITY.

LAUGH WHENEVER POSSIBLE,
AND PLAY AT BEING SERIOUS.

IF YOU HAVE FORGOTTEN
THE CREATIVE
EXPLORATIVE
CURIOUS FREEDOM
OF CHILDHOOD,
PLAY CHILDREN'S GAMES.

PEEK-A-BOO
IS AN INCREDIBLE GAME
TO PLAY WITH ADULTS,
ESPECIALLY WHEN THE OTHER PERSON
IS DROWNING IN SERIOUSNESS.

THOSE WHO
CANNOT
CHOOSE
TO PLAY
THE FOOL
ARE CONDEMNED
TO LIVE
THEIR LIVES
AS CARICATURES.

THE PROBLEM
OF LAUGHTER
IS BEST
RESOLVED
IN LAUGHING
AT THE PROBLEM.

DELIGHT IN THOSE WHO MAKE YOU ANGRY.
THEY ARE YOUR TRUE FRIENDS
WHO POINT TO THOSE VULNERABILITIES
THAT MAINTAIN YOUR VICTIMHOOD.

HAPPINESS IS NOT TO BE SOUGHT.
IT IS A BY-PRODUCT
OF HUMOROUSLY SOLVING
HUMAN PROBLEMS
AND A CONSEQUENCE
OF CONTINUOUSLY
ERODING THE BARRIERS
TO EXPERIENTIAL INTIMACY.

THE PRINCIPLE
OF
TENSION EXPLORATION

"I FEEL LIKE A DOORMAT," ANNOUNCED
ANOTHER PILGRIM ON HIS ARRIVAL.
"EVERYONE TREATS ME LIKE A DOORMAT!
WHAT SHOULD I DO?"

"PRACTICE BEING A DOORMAT TO THE FULLEST,
UNTIL YOU ARE THE BEST DOORMAT," REPLIED
THE MASTER, "THEN YOU MAY DISCOVER THERE
IS NO QUESTION."

THOSE FEELINGS
DEFINED
AND UNDERSTOOD
AS NEGATIVE
ARE EXPERIENCED
AS ALWAYS PAINFUL.

CHANGE THE DEFINITION
AND THE PAIN SOFTENS.

IT IS OFTEN
MANIFESTLY EASIER
TO REMAIN SECURED
IN ANGER
AND DEPRESSION
THAN RISK .
THE THREATENING
UNCERTAINTY
OF CHANGE.

MOST PEOPLE ARE TENSION REDUCTIVE
WITH THEMSELVES AND OTHERS.

IN REDUCING THE TENSIONS OF EXPERIENCE,
THEY AVOID PAIN AUTOMATICALLY;
OFTEN BECOMING QUITE ANGRY
AND DESTRUCTIVE
WHEN PRESSED
INTO THE EXPERIENCE
OF THEIR AGONY.

ANY EXPERIENCE OR ACTIVITY
WHICH SERVES TO AVOID TENSION
BECOMES QUITE ADDICTING.

ADDICTION AND AVOIDANCE
THEN BECOME
THE COERCIVE DIRECTORS
OF SOCIALIZING, SEX,
DRINKING, DRUGGING,
WORKING, PLAYING,
EATING, SMOKING,
THINKING
AND FANTASIZING.

ADDICTIVE BEHAVIORS
CREATE EXTREMES:
EMOTIONAL "HIGHS"
AND "LOWS."

THESE TOO
ARE ADDICTIVE.

FANTASY
CAN BE
A TOOL
OR A TOMB.

THE ULTIMATE AVOIDANCE
IS FOUND IN THE
ISOLATE SECURITY
OF FANTASY
AND PSYCHOSIS.

FACE AS MUCH EMOTIONAL PAIN AS POSSIBLE.

THE MORE YOU FACE
THE LESS THERE IS.

WHAT A BEAUTIFUL EQUATION!

WHEN YOU ARE OUT OF TOUCH
WITH YOURSELF,
YOUR FEELINGS
AND ONGOING SENSORY EXPERIENCE,
SEEK OUT ANY THERAPY
THROUGH WHICH
YOU CAN ACHIEVE
A HEALTHFUL
SELF AWARENESS.

OTHERWISE, YOU WILL HAVE
SERIOUS DIFFICULTY BECOMING
A WARM SENSITIVE PERSON
WITH YOURSELF
AND OTHERS.

GUILT,
SHAME,
ANXIETY,
JEALOUSY,
POSSESSIVENESS,
EMBARRASSMENT,
ARE AUTOMATIC
EMOTIONAL RESPONSES.

DO NOT ACT
ON THE BASIS
OF THESE FEELINGS.

EXPERIENCE THEM FULLY;
THEN ACT WITH CHOICE
AND PREFERENCE.

THROUGH THE TRAVAIL
OF CHILDHOOD
PEOPLE TOO OFTEN LOSE
THEIR RESPONSIVE JOY
AND ATTENTIVE INQUIRY
WITH THE SURROUNDING WORLD.

TO RESTORE THESE,
AS ADULTS
THEY MUST PROACT:
PLAY OUT JOY
AND ATTENTIVENESS
IN CONSCIOUS CHOICE
AND STRUGGLE.

THOSE UNWILLING
TO FACE
THEIR OWN PAIN
WILL INEVITABLY
INFLICT IT
ON OTHERS.

LET OTHERS BE RESPONSIBLE
FOR THEIR BEHAVIORS,
NOT YOUR FEELINGS.

VIGILANTLY
ACKNOWLEDGE
YOUR FEELINGS
AS YOUR OWN.

BEWARE THOSE
WHO WOULD PROTECT YOU
FROM YOUR OWN EXPERIENCE.

THE SKILL OF STRUGGLE:
  AN ABILITY
  TO CHOICEFULLY
  EXPLORE
  THE TENSION
  OF EXPERIENCE.

ACCOMPANIED WITH LOVE =
A RESPONSIBLE LEGACY.

MOST LIFESTYLES
FROM NORMAL TO PSYCHOTIC,
CONVENTIONAL TO RADICAL,
ARE CARTOONS AND CARICATURES,
CONDUCTED AUTOMATICALLY
AND REFLEXIVELY
WITHOUT CHOICE.

YOUR FIRST IMPRESSION OF SOMEONE
WILL TELL YOU HOW REFLEXIVELY
THAT PERSON RESPONDS
TO YOU AND OTHERS.

THE INITIAL CONTACT
IS OFTEN
AN AUTOMATIC
PROMISCUOUS ACTIVITY,
AVOIDING
UNFAMILIAR DISTRESS
DISCOMFORT
AND EMOTIONAL PAIN.

THE DIRECTION TO TAKE
IN ANY RELATIONSHIP
IS TOWARD
THOSE BEHAVIORS,
FEELINGS
AND TOPICS
WHICH ARE
MOST UNCOMFORTABLE.

SHARE YOUR VULNERABILITIES
AS OFTEN AS POSSIBLE
WITH OTHER PERSONS.

CONSIDER THOSE YOUR FRIENDS
WHO STIMULATE AND CARTOON
YOUR EMOTIONAL HURTS
AND SENSITIVITIES.

ACT REVERENTLY
TOWARD THEM.
THEY POINT
TO THE RESTRICTING WALLS
OF YOUR LIFE
AND INVITE YOU
TO MOVE
BEYOND THEM.

THOSE YOU LIVE WITH
AND ARE CLOSE TO
ARE POTENTIALLY
YOUR FINEST THERAPISTS.

FOR IN ADDITION TO LOVING YOU,
THEY KNOW INSTANTLY
YOUR VULNERABILITIES
AND ARE BEST ABLE
TO STIMULATE THEM.

BY AVOIDING
THEIR VULNERABILITIES,
MOST PEOPLE
MAKE LIFE
A SPECTATOR SPORT.

BEWARE THOSE
WHO PRIDE THEMSELVES
AS "REAL PEOPLE."

THEY USUALLY
TAKE THEMSELVES
AND THEIR WORDS
QUITE SERIOUSLY,
BECOMING DEADENING
WHEN NOT TAKEN
SERIOUSLY
BY OTHERS.

THE INTENSITY
OF YOUR FEELING
DOES NOT MAKE A RIGHT.

THE INTENSITY
OF YOUR ACTION
DOES NOT MAKE A TRUTH.

WHEN CHANGING WHO YOU ARE
RELY ON YOUR ACTIONS
AND YOUR INTELLECT,
NOT YOUR FEELINGS.
THEY ARE TOO CAPRICIOUS.

THE CLASSIC EXAMPLES
OF THOSE WHOSE LIVES
ARE DIRECTED
BY THEIR FEELINGS
ARE FOUND RESIDENT
IN PSYCHIATRIC HOSPITALS,
SENT THERE BY THOSE
WHO LIVE OUT THEIR LIVES
IN A LIKE MANNER.

CREATE CHOICEFUL ACTION
IN REGARD TO THOSE FEELINGS
STIMULATED BY OTHERS.

WHEN NOT SUPPORTED
BY AUTOMATIC RESPONSES,
THE COMPULSIVE QUALITY
OF FEELINGS
DISAPPEARS.

CONSIDER YOURSELF
A RIVERBED
OVER WHICH
POSITIVE
AND NEGATIVE
EXPERIENCES
FLOW.

OBSERVE THEM.
DO NOT ENMESH
YOURSELF IN THEM.

THEY ARE THE INDICATORS
NOT THE DIRECTORS
OF YOUR LIFE.

DO NOT CLING
TO NEGATIVE FEELINGS
IN MORBID INTROSPECTION.
LET GO YOUR HOLD
ON POSITIVE FEELINGS.

WHEN THE BUTTERFLY
RESTS IN YOUR HAND
DO NOT CLOSE IT.

BE AN ANTHROPOLOGIST
WITH YOUR FEELINGS.

OBSERVED,
UNDISTURBED,
THEY WILL GO
THEIR OWN WAY.
WATCHED,
UNTOUCHED,
THEY WILL PASS
ON IN THE FLOW
OF EXPERIENCE.

EACH PERSON
IS AN ACTOR
AND ACTRESS
IN SELF CHANGE.

SELF CHANGE
REQUIRES
THE ACTS OF
"AS IF."

YOU MAY ACT
"AS IF" YOU ARE
AND BECOME THAT,
OR YOU MAY ACT
"AS IF" YOU ARE
TO HIDE WHAT YOU FEEL
YOU HAVE TO BE.

AN ATTITUDE OF SELF CHANGE
OR SELF PROTECTION:
A CONSTANT CHOICE.

TO ACT
"AS IF"
IS TO BE
CHOICEFUL
IN BEHAVIOR.

TENSION EXPLORATION
FIRES THE "PHOENIX EFFECT":
A RECREATION OF THE SELF.

BE WITH YOURSELF
AS THE POTTER,
WITH WHEEL
AND HANDS
CENTERED
IN THE PRESENT MOMENT,
FORMING THE CLAY
OF YOUR OWN BEING
INTO TEN THOUSAND DESIGNS
AND COMPLEXITIES.

THE PRINCIPLE
OF
TRANSACTIONAL GAMING

THE MASTER CAME UPON A MAN
BEATING A CHILD, "TO WHAT END
DO YOU BRUTALIZE THIS CHILD?" HE INQUIRED.

"MY SON HERE HIT HIS SMALLER SISTER.
HE IS A BULLY AND I AM PUNISHING HIM!"
CAME THE ANGRY REPLY.

"OH!" SAID THE MASTER, "I SEE . . . .
YOU ARE SHOWING HIM HOW TO BE A BETTER BULLY."

YOU ARE
DEFINED BY:
  WORDS
  ACTIONS
  FEELINGS
  FANTASIES
  IMAGES
  THOUGHTS.

THESE ARE
THE TOOLS
AND ASPECTS
OF YOUR BEING.

LEFT UNATTENDED,
<u>THEY</u> WILL
DIRECT,
MANIPULATE
AND CONTROL
<u>YOU</u>.

IN LIVING,
YOU ARE
THE STEWARD
OF YOUR :
  WORDS
  ACTIONS
  FEELINGS
  FANTASIES
  IMAGES
  THOUGHTS.

HOW YOU
DEVELOP THESE
DETERMINES THE COURSE
OF YOUR RELATIONSHIP
WITH YOURSELF
AND WITH OTHERS.

A PASSAGE FRAMED
ONLY IN FEELINGS
AND FANTASIES
POINTS A LIFE
FROUGHT WITH PAIN
AND CYNICISM.

A JOURNEY DIRECTED
WITH CHOICE AND ACTION
FULFILLS THE SELF
AND CREATES JOY.

IN ORDER
FOR ALL FEELINGS
TO CONTINUE,
THEY MUST BE
STRENGTHENED
CONSTANTLY
BY WORDS
ACTIONS
FANTASIES
IMAGES
AND THOUGHTS.

SPEAK
ACT
PICTURE
IMAGINE
AND THINK
AS THE PERSON
YOU WANT TO BECOME.

WHAT YOU ARE BECOMING
IS WHO YOU ARE.

WAFFITS:
  WORDS
  ACTIONS
  FEELINGS
  FANTASIES
  IMAGES
  THOUGHTS.

WHETHER
"WAFFITS"
ARE POSITIVE
OR NEGATIVE
IS DETERMINED
BY YOUR CHOICE.

BE CAREFUL!
OR
THE "WAFFITS"
WILL GET YOU
IF YOU DON'T
WATCH OUT!

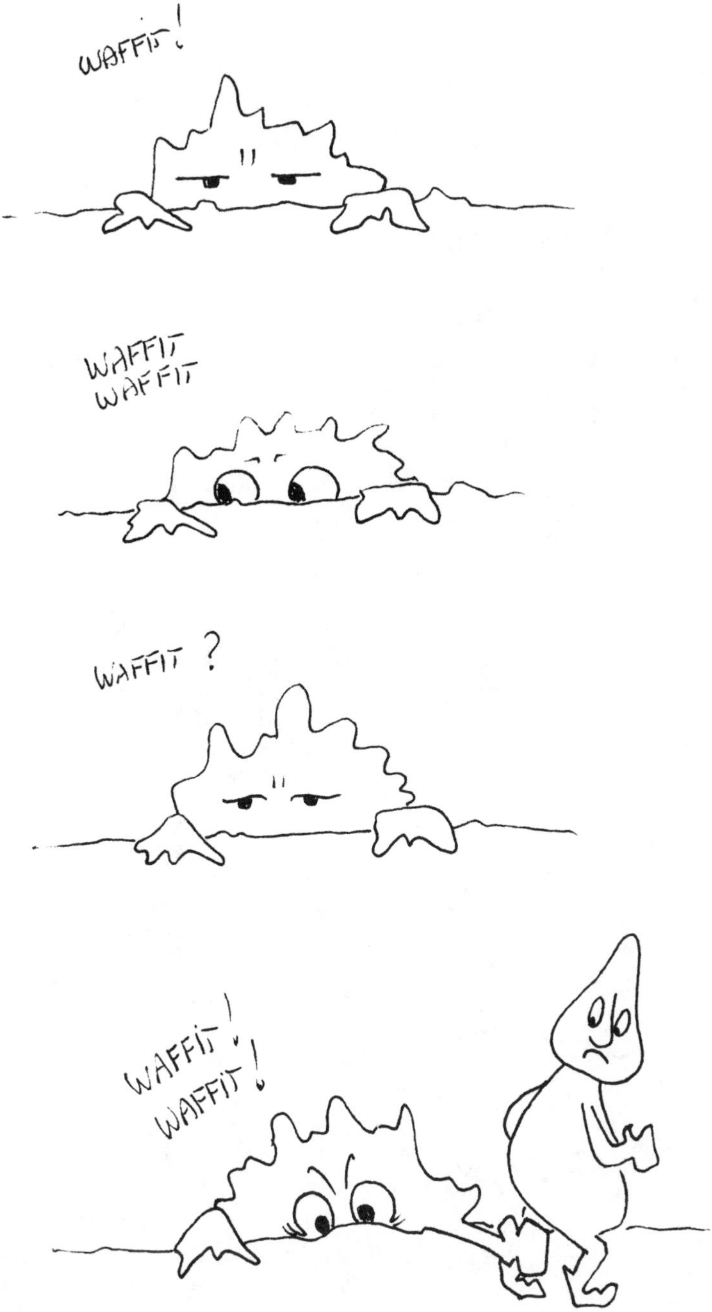
WAFFIT!
WAFFIT
WAFFIT
WAFFIT ?
WAFFIT!
WAFFIT!

YOU ARE RESPONSIBLE
FOR NO ONE
AND TO EVERYONE.

THUS IT IS YOUR CHARGE
TO ENLIGHTEN OTHERS
OF THEIR DESTRUCTIVENESS,
CARTOONING THEIR COURSE,
MODELING THEIR POSSIBILITIES.

IN EACH TRANSACTION
WITH ANOTHER,
YOU CREATE
A LIVING ART FORM,
REFLECTING
WHO YOU ARE.

BE WILLING TO EXPERIENCE
OTHER PERSONS OPENLY,
WITH NO RESTRICTIONS
ON THE EXPERIENCE.

IF THERE ARE RESTRICTIONS,
LET THEM BE THEIRS.

WHEN YOU ARE WITH OTHERS
LET THEM BE THE FOCUS,
WITH YOU AND YOUR FEELINGS
AS THE BACKGROUND.

INVITE THEM TO DO LIKEWISE
AND GENUINE MUTUALITY EMERGES.

PEOPLE OFTEN PLAY THEIR LIVES
AUTOMATICALLY AND SERIOUSLY,
WITHOUT AWARENESS.

HENCE, THEY WILL EMPLOY
PHYSICAL
SOCIAL
POLITICAL
INSTITUTIONAL
AND LEGAL POWERS
TO WIN THEIR GAMES.

SERIOUS AUTOMATIC PLAYERS
SELDOM PLAY
"I WIN, YOU WIN" GAMES.

EVEN LESS DO THEY PLAY
FOR THE ENJOYMENT
OF THE RELATIONSHIP.

DISCOVER HOW SERIOUSLY
PEOPLE WILL PERFORM
THEIR SOCIAL CONVENTIONS.

RESPOND TO THEM
IN A NON-CONVENTIONAL MANNER.

THEN BEWARE!
THEY WILL BLAME YOU
FOR "HURTING" THEM.

WHEN YOU BEHAVE NON-CONVENTIONALLY,
PEOPLE WILL ENDEAVOR TO STOP YOU
WITH SILENCE OR DISAPPROVAL,
BLAME AND EMBARRASSMENT,
COERCION AND THREAT,
DEMANDING YOU STOP PLAYING GAMES,
BE REAL AND TAKE THEM SERIOUSLY.

THIS TOO IS A GAME!

USE ALL OF YOUR EXPERIENCE
PAST, PRESENT AND FUTURE
TO FACILITATE
YOUR INVOLVEMENT
WITH OTHERS.

HOWEVER,
DO NOT ALLOW
THE GHOSTS AND PHANTOMS
OF YESTERDAY, TODAY AND TOMORROW
TO BLOCK THE INVOLVEMENT.

WHEN YOU ARE
WITH ANOTHER,
NO ONE EXISTS
EXCEPT YOU
AND THE OTHER.

NEVERTHELESS,
WHAT YOU DO
HAS EXPERIENTIAL IMPACT
FOR EVERYONE
WITHIN AND BEYOND
THE IMMEDIATE RELATIONSHIP.

AS YOU
AND THE OTHER
EFFECT EACH OTHER
SO YOU STIMULATE THE WORLD.

TEACH YOUR CHILDREN NOT TO KILL.
THAT WHICH IS KILLED
IN THE INSTANT OF DEATH
PRODUCES A KILLER,
AND ONCE DEAD
CAN NEVER REAPPEAR
FOR A LIVING RELATIONSHIP.

A FINGER
THAT PULLS A TRIGGER
IS ALL OF US,
AND KILLS
PART OF US,
REGARDLESS
OF REASON.

YOU ARE NOT INDEPENDENT
OF WHAT YOU DO.
YOU ARE REFLECTED IN IT
NO MATTER WHAT
MOTIVE OR METHOD.

IN BRINGING INJURY TO ANOTHER
YOU BRING INJURY TO YOURSELF,
FOR YOU BECOME
WHAT YOU DO.

SHOULD YOU EVER KILL ANOTHER
FOR WHATEVER REASON,
KNOW THAT YOU HAVE KILLED
A PART OF YOURSELF.

YOU BECOME WHAT YOU DO:
IN DEMEANING OTHERS YOU BECOME MEAN,
IN BRUTALIZING YOU BECOME BRUTAL,
IN HATING YOU BECOME HATEFUL,
IN KILLING YOU BECOME A KILLER.

WHAT YOU DO YOU BECOME:
IN LAUGHING YOU BECOME JOYOUS,
IN TOUCHING YOU BECOME CLOSE,
IN LOVING YOU BECOME ACCEPTING,
IN CARING YOU BECOME COMPASSIONATE.

WHATEVER YOU ARE IS STRENGTHENED
BY WHAT YOU DO AND SAY,
BY WHAT YOU THINK AND IMAGINE.

EVEN BY DEFAULT
YOU CANNOT ESCAPE
WHAT YOU BECOME.

LIKE FOOLS IN A FOG
PEOPLE RELY ON FEELINGS
FOR THEIR LIFE'S DIRECTION,
BELIEVING THE EMOTIONAL HAZE
TO BE THE LIMIT
OF THEMSELVES
AND THEIR WORLD.

CHOICE DIRECTS ACTION.
BEHAVIOR BEGETS FEELING.

LOOK THEN
TO YOUR CHOICES
AND ACTIONS
FOR THE TOOLS
OF CHANGE.

YOUR FEELINGS
ARE ONLY
REFLECTIONS
AND SHADOWS
IN THE STREAM
OF YOUR EXPERIENCE,
MERE RIPPLES IN THE RIVER.

THE PRINCIPLE
OF
PREFERENTIAL RELATEDNESS

ENCOUNTERING A MAN STRIDING BOUYANTLY
DOWN THE STREET, THE MASTER STOPPED HIM,
COMMENTING ON HOW AWKWARD HE APPEARED.
THE MAN'S SMILE WARPED INTO ANGER. "WHAT
DID YOU DO THAT FOR!" HE CRIED. "I WAS
ENJOYING MYSELF UNTIL YOU CAME ALONG."

"IT IS A CURIOUS PARADOX," SAID THE
MASTER GENTLY, "THAT TO WHICH YOU ARE
NEEDFULLY ATTACHED IS SO EASILY LOST, AND
THAT WHICH YOU PREFER IS YOURS FOREVER."

WHEN YOU ARE IN NEED OF OTHERS
YOU BECOME VICTIM TO THEM
AND TO YOUR NEEDS.

THAT WHICH YOU NEED
CONTROLS YOU.
THE NEED
THEN
BECOMES
MASTER AND MISTRESS
OF YOUR HOUSE.

WORK TO POSSESS
NO ONE AND NO THING.
THAT WHICH YOU POSSESS
DIRECTS YOU.

SEEK TO DETACH YOURSELF
FROM ALL THAT ATTRACTS
AND INVOLVES YOU.

THAT TO WHICH YOU ARE ATTACHED
CONTROLS YOU;
AND IT, NOT YOU,
DETERMINES THE PATHWAYS
OF YOUR LIFE.

IN PREFERENCE
YOU CAN
CHOOSE EXPERIENCES
AND ACTIVITIES
WHICH ARE PAINFUL
YET SELF-ENHANCING,
AND FREE YOURSELF
OF EXPERIENCES
AND ACTIVITIES
WHICH ARE EXCITING
AND COMPULSIVE,
YET SELF-DIMINISHING.

CONDITIONED EMOTIONAL RESPONSES
ARE THOSE FEELING EXPERIENCES
INEVITABLY FOLLOWED
OR REDUCED
BY AUTOMATIC,
REFLEXIVE BEHAVIORS.

THE COERCIVE CHARACTERISTICS
OF THE NEEDFUL PERSON:
  OBSESSIVE
  COMPULSIVE
  REACTIVE.

AS YOU ARE EMOTIONALLY
IN NEED OF OTHERS,
SO YOU BECOME
PARASITIC ...... A PEOPLE-HOLIC.

PEOPLE IN NEED OF PEOPLE
ARE THE VICTIMS
OF THEIR NEEDS
AND EACH OTHER.

EXPERIENTIAL LEECHING
IS A MOST DEBILITATING VICE.

TO BE IN NEED
OF OTHERS
IS TO BECOME
NEEDFUL
IN RELATIONSHIPS,
CREATING RELATIONSHIPS
FILLED BY NEEDS,
ALL OF WHICH
DEMAND FULFILLMENT
FOR THE LIFE
OF THE RELATIONSHIP.

NEEDFULNESS
FEEDS THE ROOTS
OF COERCION
AND WAR.

YOU WILL KNOW
WHEN YOU ARE IN NEED OF ANOTHER.
STRONG FEELINGS DEMAND ACTION,
AND WHEN YOU ARE UNABLE
TO ACT ON THESE FEELINGS
YOU WILL EXPERIENCE
THE PAIN OF PERSONAL LOSS.

TO LET GO OF
AND NOT ACT UPON
AN INTERPERSONAL NEED
OFTEN OPENS THE DOOR
TO A GAUNTLET
OF EMOTIONAL PAIN,
WHICH MUST BE RUN.

TO KEEP HOLD OF
AND RETAIN
AN INTERPERSONAL NEED
SETS THE STAGE
FOR A LIFE OF
NEVER-ENDING CRISES,
CONFLICTS AND EMOTIONAL PAIN.

WHEN DISALLOWED,
A NEED
IS MOST CLEARLY RECOGNIZED
BY ITS EMOTIONAL ACCOMPANIMENT.

THIS ORCHESTRATION OF INJURY
WILL DISSOLVE
AS THE EMOTIONS ARE EXPERIENCED
TO THEIR FULLEST
IN THE COMPANY OF
PREFERENTIAL BEHAVIORS.

UNBELTING THE BONDAGE
OF NEGATIVE FEELINGS
AND EMOTIONS
IS A MOST ENLIGHTENING
EXPERIENCE.

KNOW ALSO
THAT LETTING GO,
EVEN OF PHYSICAL PAIN,
RELEASES THE TEARS
AND TOXINS
OF WITHDRAWAL.

A NEEDFUL ATTACHMENT
TO ONE 'S STRONG FEELINGS
LEADS TO A LIFE
OF WORRY
OVER THEIR LOSS.

LEARN TO EXPERIENCE
EACH NEED
WHILE ACTING
IN PREFERENCE
AND CHOICE.

WHEN NOT ACTED UPON,
BOTH NEEDFULNESS
AND ITS EMOTIONAL CORTEGE
DISAPPEAR.

WHEN YOU ARE
WITH OTHERS
IN PREFERENCE
YOU HAVE NO NEED
TO CONTROL THEM.

TO THE EXTENT
THAT YOU ARE
NOT IN NEED
OF ANY ONE
OR ANY THING,
SO ARE YOU TRULY FREE
TO LOVE AND CARE
FOR YOURSELF
AND ALL PERSONS,
FOR ALL LIVING THINGS
AND THE UNIVERSE.

NON-ATTACHMENT
DOES NOT EQUAL
NON-COMMITMENT.

EACH LIFE
IS A DRAMA
ILLUSTRATING
AN ARRAY
OF WORDS
ACTIONS
FEELINGS
FANTASIES
IMAGES
THOUGHTS.

LET EVERY BEHAVIOR
FROM CONVENTIONAL
TO PSYCHOTIC,
TRADITIONAL
TO RADICAL,
WHETHER YOURS
OR ANOTHERS,
BE AN OPTION
IN YOUR REPERTOIRE
OF POSSIBILITIES.

FREEDOM
IS EXTANT
IN THE POTENTIAL
OF ALL POSSIBILITIES.

EACH PERSON
YOU ENCOUNTER
IS YOUR TEACHER,
ESPECIALLY THOSE PERSONS
YOU DISLIKE OR HATE.
THEY IN PARTICULAR
PRESENT YOU THE OPPORTUNITY
TO FREE YOURSELF
OF YOUR ATTACHMENT
TO HATRED.

LET GO YOUR ANGER
AND IRRITATION
TOWARD OTHERS,
OR YOU WILL WALK
ALWAYS IN THEIR SHADOW.

A MOST PRECIOUS GIFT:
ALLOWING OTHERS
TO EXPERIENCE
ONES'S VULNERABILITIES,
AND THEN
TO REACH OUT
THROUGH THIS AGONY
TO TOUCH THEIR REALITY.

BECAUSE YOU AND ANOTHER
ARRIVE AT NON-NEEDFULNESS
IN YOUR RELATIONSHIP,
IS NOT AN ASSURITY
THAT YOUR PREFERENCES
WILL OVERLAP.

SOMETIMES
GEARS DON'T MESH.

                         AT TIMES
                         PREFERENCES
                         AND PRIORITIES
                         ARE DIFFERENT
                         AND CONFLICT.

WHERE OVERLAP OF PREFERENCES
IS NOT SUFFICIENT,
PEOPLE CANNOT LIVE TOGETHER.

COSMIC RELATIONSHIPS
ARE NOT ALWAYS POSSIBLE.

SOMETIMES
A CUP OF TEA
TOGETHER
IS ALL-THAT-IS.

IN AN UNWANTED
INTERPERSONAL
OR SOCIAL
SITUATION,
THESE CHOICES:
   CHANGE IT (FIRST)!
   LIVE IT (SECOND)!
   LEAVE IT (THIRD)!

RELATIONSHIPS
ARE NOT FOUND.
THEY ARE CREATED.

UNLESS YOU GRANT EQUAL IMPORTANCE
TO GARBAGE AND SUNSETS,
YOU WILL BE DESTRUCTIVE
WITH THOSE ASPECTS OF LIFE
YOU CONSIDER WORTHLESS.

THIS, HOWEVER, DOES NOT MEAN
THAT YOU MUST PREFER
GARBAGE OVER SUNSETS.

THAT WHICH YOU MUST AVOID
AND CANNOT BE,
EVEN IN FANTASY,
DIRECTS AND CONTROLS YOU.

THEREFORE,
PRACTICE IMAGINING
AND CREATING FANTASIES
OF THE MOST AWFUL AND HEINOUS ACTS
THAT COULD BE DONE BY YOU
TO YOURSELF,
OTHERS
AND THE WORLD.

IN THE FANTASY OF THESE THINGS
YOU CAN DISCOVER
THE FREEDOM NOT TO DO THEM
AND ESCAPE THE REFLEXIVE ACT
OF DOING GOOD.

THE ABILITY TO LIE,
TO STAND FREE
FROM THE IMPERATIVE
AUTOMATIC
POINT OF VIEW,
IS A FIRST STEP
IN TRANSCENDANCE.

THEN
TO STEP BOLDLY BEYOND
THE COMPASSED CAVERN
OF ME AND MINE,
INTO THE UNBOUNDED
ELEMENTAL
PANORAMA
OF AN ABSURD UNIVERSE,
AND THERE
TO FREELY CREATE
AND PLAY
ALL THE FACETS
OF EXPERIENCE.

THIS IS FREEDOM
LAUGHING
AT THE WIND.

AT TIMES
CHOOSE TO BE
AWAY FROM OTHERS
TO EXPERIENCE YOURSELF
ALONE IN THE NON-PERSON WORLD.

EXPLORE YOUR LONELINESS
WHENEVER POSSIBLE.
IT IS NOT A BOTTOMLESS PIT
BUT A BRIDGE
TO THE EXPERIENCE
OF COMPLETE UNION
WITH THE WORLD.

WITHIN ALONENESS
RESTS THE RECOGNITION
OF ONE'S SINGULARITY
INTEGRATED WITH ALL-THAT-IS.

SENSUALITY
AND SEXUALITY

THEN CAME ANOTHER PILGRIM, BLUSHING.
HE ASKED THE MASTER TO SPEAK OF
INTIMACY AND SEX.

"AH," SAID THE MASTER, NODDING.
"YOU WISH ME TO VIOLATE YOUR TABOOS.
THAT WHICH MUST NOT BE SEEN, CANNOT
BE LOOKED AT. THAT WHICH MUST BE KEPT
SILENT, CANNOT BE HEARD. THAT WHICH
MUST NOT BE SAID, CANNOT BE SPOKEN OF!"

SEXUAL FREEDOM
DOES NOT CONDONE
SEXUAL PROMISCUITY.

SEXUAL FREEDOM
IS DIRECTED
TOWARD EXPERIENCING
THE UNIQUENESS OF THE OTHER
IN AN ATTITUDE
OF MUTUAL ENHANCEMENT
WITH MUTUAL CONSENT.

SEX
MUST ALSO
BE AN ACT OF ECOLOGY.

WHERE SEXUAL DISEASE
RUNS RAMPANT,
EACH PARTICIPANT
HAS A RESPONSIBILITY
FOR THE HEALTH
OF ALL PARTICIPANTS.

PREFERENTIAL INTIMACY
BRINGS TO A RELATIONSHIP
THE CHOICE
BETWEEN AND WITHIN
SENSUALITY AND SEXUALITY.

SENSUALITY
IS INTERPERSONAL
AND PHYSICAL CONTACT
WITHOUT THE NECESSITY
OF SEXUAL ACTIVITY.

SENSUALITY
INVITES EACH PERSON
INTO THE INTIMATE EXPERIENCE
OF ALL FEELINGS
BETWEEN ALL PERSONS,
REGARDLESS OF GENDER.

EACH PERSON
IS CAPABLE
OF HAVING
THOUSANDS
OF DIFFERENT
LOVERS.

SEXUAL EXCLUSION
INCORPORATES
THE SEEDS OF
INTERPERSONAL
AGGRESSION
AND WAR.

WHEN YOU HAVE GROWN
THROUGH SEXUAL NEEDFULNESS
TO SEXUAL PREFERENCE,
YOU WILL DISCOVER
THERE ARE
MANY MORE PEOPLE
TO SHARE AND ENJOY
SEXUALLY.

THE PREFERENTIAL HEART
HAS MANY ROOMS!

SEXUALITY,
LIKE ANY EXPRESSION
OF THE HUMAN CONDITION,
CAN BE PERFORMED
IN A CONTEXT
OF CARING CONCERN
FOR THE OTHER,
OR IT CAN BE
ISOLATED
AND COMPARTMENTALIZED
WITHIN ONESELF
ALONE.

WHEN PEOPLE BECOME EROTIC
THEY OFTEN BECOME "SPERM BLIND,"
NOT SEEING OTHERS
IN ALL THEIR ASSETS
AND LIABILITIES.

TOO OFTEN
PEOPLE USE
EACH OTHER
AS TOILETS,
CAVITIES
AND DILDOES.

SEXUAL RELATIONSHIPS
WITH PERSONS
OF THE SAME
OR OPPOSITE
GENDER
HAVE VITALITY
ONLY WHEN THEY ARE OPEN
TO THE LOVE,
SENSUALITY
AND SEXUALITY
OF OTHERS.

CLOSED RELATIONSHIPS
WHICH DISALLOW
EVEN A MINIMUM
OF EXPERIENTIAL INTIMACY
WITH OTHER PERSONS
WILL EVENTUATE
AS SEQUESTERED PRISONS
STIFLING THOSE INVOLVED.

AN OPEN RELATIONSHIP
MUST INCLUDE
A WILLINGNESS
TO EXPERIENCE
AND EXPLORE
THE TENSIONS OF
SUCH STRESSFUL EMOTIONS
AS JEALOUSY
AND POSSESSIVENESS.

WHEN EXPERIENCED FULLY
IN THE COMPANY OF
PREFERENTIAL ACTIONS,
THESE EMOTIONS GIVE WAY
TO FEELINGS
OF CORPORATE LOVE
AND CARING.

LET SEXUAL RELATIONSHIPS
BE A PUBLIC MATTER.

SOMETHING
SO POWERFUL
AND CREATIVE
AS SEXUALITY
SHOULD NOT
BE COMPULSIVELY
HIDDEN.

WHEN LOVE AND SEX
ARE PUBLICALLY
COUNTENANCED,
PEOPLE WILL
MORE ACTIVELY
UNDERSTAND
WHAT IT MEANS
TO GROW BEYOND
"COCK 'N CUNT"
IN THEIR RELATIONSHIPS.

MOST PEOPLE
REFLEXIVELY
KEEP SEX
A PRIVATE MATTER.

NEEDFULLY
THEY MAKE IT SO,
DEFENDING
THEIR POSITION
IN ANGER
AND ROMANCE
WITH STATEMENTS
SUCH AS:
"SEX IS A PERSONAL MATTER."
"THE LOVE BETWEEN TWO PEOPLE
CANNOT BE SHARED WITH OTHERS."
"CHILDREN WILL BE TRAUMATIZED
IF THEY SEE THEIR PARENTS MAKE LOVE."

WHETHER
EXPRESSIONS
OF INTIMACY,
SENSUALITY
AND SEXUALITY
OCCUR IN THE PRIVATE
OR PUBLIC DOMAIN,
SHOULD BE
FOR THE PERSONS INVOLVED
A MATTER OF CONVENIENCE
AND PREFERENTIAL
AGREEMENT.

IN A SOCIALLY EVOLVED WORLD
WHERE PEOPLE ARE
CONTINUOUSLY EXPLORING
THEIR OWN
AND OTHERS'
WAYS OF BEING,
AND ARE PLAYFULLY
SEARCHING
EACH OTHER'S VULNERABILITIES,
THE HUMORFUL MODELING
OF LOVE AND SEX
FOR CHILDREN
WOULD BE A MOST
NATURAL ACTIVITY.

THE BEDROOM DOOR
SHOULD NOT BE
REFLEXIVELY
AND AUTOMATICALLY
CLOSED TO CHILDREN.

WITH CHILDREN,
WHAT CANNOT BE SEEN
AND CANNOT BE SPOKEN OF
IS OFTEN RELEGATED
TO THEIR FEAR-FILLED
AND MAGICAL
FANTASIES.

ANY HUMAN BEHAVIOR,
BE IT LOVE, AFFECTION,
HATE, FEAR,
SEX OR DEATH,
WHICH CANNOT BE EXPLORED
IN THE HEALING LIGHT OF DAY,
IS REMANDED
TO THE RITUALS
OF IGNORANCE
PREJUDICE
SUPERSTITION
AND PORNOGRAPHY.

IN A SANE
AND HEALTHFUL
SOCIETY,
LOVE,
AFFECTION
AND SEX BREAKS
WOULD BE A PART
OF ANY WORK
AND SOCIAL SITUATION.

IN A PUSH BUTTON WORLD
CONTRIVED OF STRESS,
CONFLICT AND WAR,
THE ONGOING EROSION
OF HUMAN COMPASSION
BECOMES THE EXPERIENCE
OF ETERNAL DISASTER,
SPAWNING DEPRESSION,
RAGE, REVOLUTION
AND THE REFLEXIVE RUT
FOR THE IMMEDIACY
OF INSTANT ORGASM.

DEATH

SEEING A FUNERAL, THE MASTER CLAPPED
AND CHEERED.

"HAVE YOU NO COMPASSION FOR THE DEAD?"
A MOURNER SHOUTED ANGRILY.

"THE PLAY IS OVER," AMUSED THE MASTER.

TO THE LOST
THE ZTT MASTER
IS A BEACON.

TO THE SORROWING
THE ZTT MASTER
IS A GRACEFUL
COMPANION.

TO THE DISCONSOLATE
THE ZTT MASTER
OFFERS A GUMDROP.

DEATH
IS YOUR CONSTANT
COMPANION.

AT ANY MOMENT
IT MAY REACH OUT
AND TOUCH
YOUR MORTALITY.

THE ENJOYMENT
OF THE WORLD
IS ALWAYS
A SHARED EXPERIENCE.

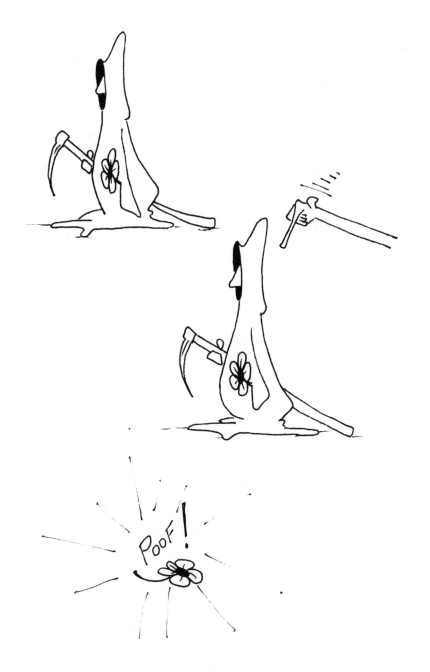

POOF!

DEATH
IS THE COMMONER
OF ALL THINGS.

NONE
MAY WITHOLD
THEIR PASSAGE.

THE DENIAL
OF DEATH
IS THE ACTIVITY
OF ONE APPROACHING
WINTER WITH A MATCH.

GRAVITY,
STIFFNESS
AND NECESSITY
ARE ASPECTS
OF THE DEAD.

THEREFORE,
MAKE HUMOR,
PLAYFULNESS
AND COMPASSION
YOUR COMPANIONS
IN GRIEF.

LAUGHTER,
ACTIVITY
AND GRACE
ARE MANNERS
OF THE LIVING.

BETTER AN OPEN HAND
THEN A CLOSED FIST
IN THE FACE OF DEATH.

THE TASK IS ONE
OF LETTING GO
AND REACHING OUT,
RATHER THAN
HOLDING ON
AND FENDING OFF.

TO EQUATE
DEATH
ONLY
WITH LOSS
IS TO LOSE
LIFE.

FOR SURELY
SPRING
UNFOLDS
ONLY
FROM THE ROOTS
OF WINTER.

BIRTH
AND DEATH
ARE THE GATES
IN NATURE'S GARDEN.

THOSE NEEDFULLY
ATTACHED
TO THE WORLD,
WILL ALWAYS
TAKE LIFE
AND DEATH
PERSONALLY.

ZTT GAMING

"I JUST WANT TO BE ME!" ANNOUNCED
THE PILGRIM EMPHATICALLY. "HOW CAN
I BE MYSELF?"

THE MASTER YAWNED AND WROTE FOR THE
PILGRIM THE FOLLOWING PRESCRIPTION:
  "PLAY AT BEING YOU FOR ONE YEAR.
  PLAY AT BEING NOT YOU FOR THE
  NEXT YEAR. IF AT THE END OF THESE
  TWO YEARS YOU STILL HAVE THE
  QUESTION, PLAY AT BEING SOMEONE
  ELSE, SINCE YOU OBVIOUSLY DO
  NOT WISH TO BE YOU."

133

ZTT IS A METAGAME.
IT PROVIDES
A PHILOSOPHICAL
AND BEHAVIORAL
FRAMEWORK
WITHIN WHICH
ALL OTHER GAMES
ARE PLAYED.

THAT EACH OF US
IS GAMING
IS NOT A NEW CONCEPT.

IN ZTT,
HOWEVER,
THE PLAYERS
DISCIPLINE THEMSELVES
TO PLAY KINETICALLY,
MANIPULATING WITHOUT PAUSE
TO INTERRUPT, DISRUPT
AND CHANGE THE COURSE
OF THEIR OWN AND OTHERS'
DESTRUCTIVE GAMING.

IN THEIR ADHERENCE
TO THE PRINCIPLES,
ZTT PLAYERS
ACTIVELY HOLD
TO THE GUIDELINES
OF TAKING NEITHER
THEMSELVES
OR ZTT
SO SERIOUSLY
AS TO BE INJURIOUS,
SO IMPORTANT
AS TO BE COERCIVE,
SO RIGHTEOUS
AS TO BE DOGMATIC,
OR SO CONCRETELY
AS TO BE RIGID
AND UNBENDING.

ABOVE ALL,
ZTT PLAYERS
SCHOOL
IN HUMOR,
BEING ABLE
TO LAUGH
EQUALLY
AT THEMSELVES,
ZTT
AND THE WORLD.

ZTT PLAYERS
ARE SOCIOTHERAPISTS:
ACTIVE
HUMORFUL
PREFERENTIAL
PLAYERS OF LIFE
AND LIVING,
CONTINUALLY TRANSACTING
IN PLAYFUL EXPLORATION
AND CHOICEFUL CONDUCT
OF THEIR OWN
AND OTHERS'
WAYS OF BEING.

FOR A ZTT PLAYER
THERE ARE MANY WAYS
TO INTERRUPT
AND PLAY WITH
AUTOMATIC, CONCRETE
AND REFLEXIVE
WAYS OF ACTING
AND THINKING.

FOR EXAMPLE,
EXPLORE AND
HUMORFULLY PLAY
WITH YOUR OWN
AND OTHERS'
DESTRUCTIVE
ACTIONS AND SPEECH
IN THE FOLLOWING WAYS:

... EXAGGERATE THE OTHER PERSON'S
   GESTURES, TONE OF VOICE,
   MANNER OF SPEECH OR ACTIONS.

      ... CREATE DISSONANCE
         IN COMMUNICATION BY
         VARYING YOUR VERBAL CONTENT,
         EYE CONTACT, FACIAL EXPRESSION,
         VOICE (TONE, VOLUME, CLARITY, ETC.),
         BODY POSTURE, HAND GESTURES,
         OR PHYSICAL DISTANCE.

         DO THESE SINGLY OR IN COMBINATION,
         CREATING A HUMOR FILLED KOAN
         FOR THE OTHER PERSON(S) TO SOLVE.

... RESPOND TO THE OTHER WITH
   DEFINITE PAUSES
   OR STUTTERING.

            ... TURN YOUR BACK TO A PERSON
               WHO IS COMMUNICATING
               DESTRUCTIVELY WITH YOU.

... ABRUPTLY EXCUSE YOURSELF
AND WALK AWAY IN THE MIDDLE
OF A CONVERSATION.

      ... WITH COMPULSIVE TALKERS,
      FACETIOUSLY DISMISS THEM
      WITH THE STATEMENT THAT
      WHAT THEY ARE SAYING
      IS UNIMPORTANT.
      IF THEY BEGIN TO WALK AWAY,
      TELL THEM YOU HAVE RECONSIDERED
      AND ASK THEM TO RETURN.
      THEN DISMISS THEM AGAIN.

... WITH THE CONSTANT COMPLAINER,
DEMAND EQUAL TIME
TO VOICE YOUR COMPLAINTS.

      ... WITH THE CHRONICALLY "HELPLESS,"
      ANNOUNCE THAT YOU ARE TIRED
      OF HELPING AND THAT THEY MUST NOW
      HELP YOU FOR A CHANGE.

. . . IN THE FACE OF SERIOUSNESS,
LAUGH AND CONTINUE LAUGHING,
EVEN IF YOU DON'T FEEL LIKE IT.

REMEMBER, FEELINGS OF HUMOR
WILL FOLLOW LAUGHTER,
JUST AS LAUGHTER
FOLLOWS FEELINGS OF HUMOR.

. . . MIX IN EQUAL PARTS
SERIOUS AND HUMORFUL
RESPONSES
TO ANY SERIOUS INQUIRY.

. . . WITH THE UNENDING "SAD STORY" TELLERS,
BEGIN AN EXAGGERATED SOBBING
AND IN TEARS TELL THEM
THAT SUCH A SAD STORY
DESERVES ALL THE PITY
IN THE WORLD.

... HUMOROUSLY DESCRIBE
SOMEONE'S REFLEXIVE WAY
OF RELATING
AS "PSYCHOPATHOLOGY."
FACETIOUSLY INVITE OTHERS
TO PRACTICE THIS BEHAVIOR
SO THAT THEY CAN LEARN HOW
NOT TO DO IT.

> ... WITH PERSONS WHO ALWAYS
> ARE HAVING "BAD DAYS,"
> ASK THEM TO GIVE YOU
> A DETAILED DESCRIPTION
> OF HOW THEY CREATE
> SUCH ROTTEN DAYS.
> THEN INVITE THEM
> TO WORK HARDER
> AT CREATING
> THE BEST "BAD DAY."

... WITH A GROUP OF PEOPLE,
SWITCH FROM PERSON TO PERSON
IN THE MIDDLE OF SENTENCES,
CHANGING THE SUBJECT,
LEAVING EACH PERSON WITH A
"HANGING IN THE AIR" KOAN.
SHOULD ANYONE COMMENT
ON YOUR RUDENESS, THANK THEM
FOR THE COMPLIMENT.

      ... TO THE "COMPLAINER,"
      WONDER ALOUD AND MIRTHFULLY
      AS TO WHY YOU MUST BE SUBJECT
      TO SUCH MISERABLE CONVERSATION,
      ESPECIALLY SINCE YOU HAVE EVOLVED
      TO A "HIGHER PLANE OF EXISTENCE."
      THEN ASK WHY
      THIS PERSON IS
      PUNISHING YOU
      WITH HIS PRESENCE.

DISRUPTION GAMES
ARE CONDUCTED
HUMORFULLY,
WITH PLAYFUL
AND GENUINE CONCERN
FOR THE HEALTHFUL
GROWTH OF ALL PERSONS.

THE INABILITY TO PLAY
HUMORFULLY,
CAN BE ATTRIBUTED
TO A DEFECT
OF THE SPINAL COLUMN
KNOWN AS
HAVING BACK BONE.
ASSOCIATED SYMPTOMS
ARE THE STIFF UPPER LIP
AND SOCKS
THAT WON'T FALL DOWN.

IT IS EQUALLY IMPORTANT
TO INTERRUPT
NEEDFUL ATTACHMENTS
TO POSITIVE AND "GOOD"
FEELINGS, BEHAVIORS
AND EXPERIENCES.

FOR EXAMPLE:
... PLAY SERIOUSLY
   AT STRIVING TO CREATE
   A FUN-FILLED RELAXING DAY.

                ... EXPRESS DISMAY AND SADNESS
                    THAT ANOTHER FEELS SO GOOD.
                    GIVE THEM YOUR CONDOLENCES.

... PLAY THE ROLE OF "CONTRARY."
   ACT CONTRARY
   TO YOUR POSITIVE FEELINGS
   FOR ONE DAY.
   THEN ACT CONTRARY
   TO YOUR NEGATIVE FEELINGS.

                ... PLAY AT BEING IN A GOOD MOOD.
                    LAUGH, SMILE AND ACT HAPPY,
                    REGARDLESS OF HOW YOU FEEL.

... INVITE THE ECSTATIC PERSON
   TO DO NOTHING UNTIL
   THE FEELINGS OF EXUBERANCE
   SUBSIDE.

                ... WITH THE INEVITABLE
                    "FUN" PERSON,
                    ACT BORED.

REMEMBER,
THAT WHICH YOU NEED,
WHETHER FEELINGS, IDEAS,
BEHAVIORS OR PERSONS,
WILL INEVITABLY
CONTROL YOU,
FOR YOU MUST
EXPEND ENERGY
AND CONCENTRATION
ON SATISFYING
THAT NEED.

COMPULSIVE
AND NEEDFUL
ATTACHMENTS
PRODUCE
VICTIMS.

YOU BECOME VICTIM
TO ANY BEHAVIOR,
THOUGHT OR ACTION
WHICH MUST BE COMPULSIVELY
AND REFLEXIVELY PERFORMED
IN THE SERVICE
OF A NEED.

147

A CONSTANT GOAL
IN ZTT GAMING
IS TO CREATE
THE FREEDOM TO ACT
PURPOSEFULLY
FROM PREFERENCE
RATHER THAN
REFLEXIVELY
FROM HABIT.

SO MUCH
OF HUMAN CONTACT
IS CONDUCTED
AUTOMATICALLY
WITH LITTLE THOUGHT
OR FEELING.

WE ARE
TOO OFTEN
EACH OTHER'S
HABITS.

THE EXPERIENCE
YOU HOLD TO
IMPRISONS YOU
IN THE FANTASY
OF WHAT WAS
AND WHAT MIGHT
HAVE BEEN.

REFLEXIVE AND AUTOMATIC BEHAVIORS
CONFINE THE FLOW OF EXPERIENCE.

TO REMAIN UNSHACKLED
IN THE IMMEDIACY
OF THE PRESENT EXPERIENCE,
PRACTICE SWITCHING FOCUS.

ALLOW YOUR ATTENTION
TO SCAN THE FIELD
OF EXPERIENCE
AMONGST AND BETWEEN
PEOPLE
SITUATIONS
EVENTS
THINGS
THOUGHTS
FEELINGS
FANTASIES
AND MEMORIES.

THAT WHICH
HOLDS YOUR ATTENTION
CONTROLS YOUR ATTENITON!

TO ASSIST YOURSELF AND OTHERS
DISRUPT REFLEXIVE FIXATIONS,
SWITCH THE FOCUS AND FACT
OF YOUR ATTENTION
IN RESPONSE TO THEM
AND THE SITUATION.

WHEN NEXT YOU ARE
IN CONFLICT WITH ANOTHER,
FOR EXAMPLE,
SWITCH FOCUS FROM YOUR ANGER
TO YOUR APPRECIATION
OF THE OTHER PERSON,
AND SHARE THAT WITH THEM.

PEOPLE WILL OFTEN
FIXATE THEIR ATTENTION
IN THE PROPER PROCEDURE
OF A SOCIAL CONVENTION
AS AN AVOIDANCE
OF SOCIAL TENSION.

THE SERIOUSNESS
AND RIGIDITY
OF TENSION AVOIDANCE
CAN BE INTERRUPTED
BY TAKING THE CONVENTION
AND RITUAL
LITERALLY
AND HUMORFULLY.

BECOME PLAYFUL
WITH CONVENTION.
FOR EXAMPLE:
. . . BEFORE RESPONDING,
    BE AS THE CHILD
    WHO TAKES A LONG
    AND QUIET
    UNEMOTIONAL LOOK
    AT THE OTHER PERSON.

        . . . OR ACCEPT THE OPTION TO REFUSE
            WHEN A REQUEST IS DELIVERED
            AS A SOCIAL QUESTION.

. . . PERHAPS, SHAKE HANDS
    WITH THE OPPOSITE HAND
    OR NOT AT ALL.

        . . . WHEN ASKED "HOW ARE YOU?"
            TAKE HOLD OF THE OTHER PERSON,
            THANK THEM PROFUSELY FOR THEIR INQUIRY,
            AND TELL THEM HOW YOU ARE, IN DETAIL!

THIS DOES NOT MEAN
EVERY SOCIAL CONVENTION,
RITE AND RITUAL
IS TENSION REDUCTIVE
OR IS TO BE DISRUPTED.

BEWARE THOSE
WHO WILL TAKE A GUIDELINE
AND MAKE OF IT AN IMPERATIVE RULE.

THE VALUE
OF TEN THOUSAND WORDS
IS NO MORE
AND NO LESS
THAN THE ACTIONS
OF THEIR AUTHOR.

AFTERWORD.

WITH EACH STEP
IS THE RISK OF FALLING.

IN FALLING
IS THE POSSIBILITY OF LOSS.

IN LOSS
IS THE EXPERIENCE OF PAIN.

IN PAIN
IS THE DISCOVERY OF AWARENESS.

IN AWARENESS
IS SELF-KNOWLEDGE.

IN SELF-KNOWLEDGE
IS THE POTENTIAL OF BEING.

IN BEING
IS BECOMING

IN BECOMING
IS MOVEMENT.

IN MOVEMENT
IS THE RISK OF FALLING.

WITH EACH STEP
 A   LIFE UNFOLDS
AND RETURNS.

ROBERT M. ANTHONY, PH.D. IS A CLINICAL PSYCHOLOGIST (PB3398) AND MARRIAGE, FAMILY AND CHILD COUNSELOR (MK 2499) IN PRIVATE PRACTICE IN ORANGE COUNTY, CALIFORNIA. HE IS THE FOUNDER OF ZEN TRANSACTIONAL THERAPY (ZTT), FIRST PUBLISHED AS A PROFESSIONAL ARTICLE IN *CREATIVE PSYCHOTHERAPY: A SOURCE BOOK,* UNIVERSITY ASSOCIATES, LA JOLLA, 1976.

J. DIGBY HENRY IS A PSYCHOTHERAPIST (MK7057), ENVIRONMENTAL PSYCHOLOGIST AND HUMAN RELATIONS TRAINING CONSULTANT. HE IS CO-WRITER AND ILLUSTRATOR OF ZTT. HE CAN BE FOUND LIVING AND PLAYING ZTT IN THE UNITED STATES' SOUTHWEST.

To order additional copies
of ZEN Transactional Therapy,
send $11.95 (includes $1.00 for
postage).

California Residents Please Add
6 1/2 % Sales Tax (72 cents)
for each book ordered.
Total for Ca. Residents - $12.67.
Thank you.

Please send me _____ copies.

Enclosed find _____

name _____

address _____

city/state/zip_____

Please make all checks payable to:
Fragments West, 2705 East Seventh Street,
Long Beach, California 90814

To order additional copies
of ZEN Transactional Therapy,
send $11.95 (includes $1.00 for
postage).

California Residents Please Add
6 1/2 % Sales Tax (72 cents)
for each book ordered.
Total for Ca. Residents - $12.67.
Thank you.

Please send me _____ copies.

Enclosed find _____

name _____

address _____

city/state/zip_____

Please make all checks payable to:
Fragments West, 2705 East Seventh Street,
Long Beach, California 90814